Everything Women know about Business, Religion, Sports, Politics, and Sex

Dr. I. M. Apigg, Ph.D.

ISBN: 0975465627
ISBN-13: 978-0-9754656-2-2

DEDICATION

To the woman that I love and seek to understand

Everything Women know about Business, Religion, Sports, Politics, and Sex

Everything Women know about Business, Religion, Sports, Politics, and Sex

ABOUT THE AUTHOR

Dr. I. M. Apigg is an accomplished author and academic as well as an outspoken supporter of feminism. He studied abroad for several years during his exhaustive research into the female psyche. After observing the women's movement for over 25 years, he finally settled down to write and teach at the university level. He is a tireless advocate for social equality and women's rights. It is his wish that the release of this seminal work improves male/female relationships around the world.

www.ingramcontent.com/pod-product-compliance
Lightning Source LLC
Chambersburg PA
CBHW050536280326
41933CB00011B/1613
* 9 7 8 0 9 7 5 4 6 5 6 2 2 *